HEAVEN SPEAKS TO THOSE WHO STRUGGLE TO FORGIVE

Direction for Our Times
As given to Anne, a lay apostle

Heaven Speaks to Those Who Struggle to Forgive

Direction for Our Times
As given to Anne, a lay apostle

ISBN: 978-1-933684-36-9

© Copyright 2007-2009 Direction for Our Times. All rights reserved. No part of this book may be used or reproduced in any manner whatsoever without written permission.

Publisher:
Direction for Our Times
9000 West 81st Street
Justice, IL 60458
708-496-9300

www.directionforourtimes.org

Direction for Our Times is a 501(c)(3) tax-exempt organization.

Manufactured in the United States of America

Direction for Our Times wishes to manifest its complete obedience and submission of mind and heart to the final and definitive judgment of the Magisterium of the Catholic Church and the local Ordinary regarding the supernatural character of the messages received by Anne, a lay apostle.

In this spirit, the messages of Anne, a lay apostle, have been submitted to her bishop, Most Reverend Leo O'Reilly, Bishop of Kilmore, Ireland, and to the Vatican Congregation for the Doctrine of the Faith for formal examination. In the meantime Bishop O'Reilly has given permission for their publication.

Table of Contents

December 13, 2006
  Jesus 1
  St. Faustina 3
  St. Faustina 7
  St. Faustina 9
  Blessed Mother 13

December 13, 2006
Jesus

How blessed I am that you take a moment to read these words. I am God. I am complete, and yet your simple act of reading My words gives Me glory. You are important to Me and you are important to My family, which includes all men of good will. Because I love you and because I need your help, I wish to give you the opportunity to find greater peace in your heart. It is clear to Me that many suffer from hidden wounds. The only way for these wounds to heal is for the carrier of the wound to forgive the one who inflicted the injury. My dear child, this can be difficult. When a wound finds a home in the heart, it becomes comfortable there. It must be loosened and shifted. Both a willingness to forgive and a spirit of forgiveness are necessary because it is these things that make the wound uncomfortable. The wound then begins to dislodge. This reawakens the pain, but only temporarily until the wound is removed altogether.

I want to begin this process in you. If you proceed in the process of forgiveness with Me, you will find that forgiveness floods your heart. Your wounds will be gone. I have the power to heal every one of your wounds. When you try to do this alone, you do not experience success and you find that bitterness persists. Bitterness characterizes My enemy. Forgiveness characterizes Me. You, a beloved little child of God, seek to find peace in your heart. You will only find peace if you step into the stream of goodness. This stream is like a river of grace with which I desire to bathe you, removing all pain and injury. What will remain in your soul is joy. This joy, this heavenly peace, will be obtained by accepting your flaws and accepting the flaws of others. You see, My friend, if you accept the flaws and sins of others, you will soften in attitude toward yourself. I love you. I accept you. I need you to accept yourself so that you will be at peace in My Kingdom and it is through forgiving others that you will find acceptance of your own humanity.

St. Faustina

Oh my, how we suffer on earth. We are so very woundable, are we not? Our humanity makes us vulnerable and we are subject to pain. My friends, Jesus wishes to heal you from the injuries levied against you. It is possible that you are suffering from pains that were inflicted in the past. At this time, Jesus is allotting a torrent of graces because He wants His little ones to be at peace. If a person is at peace, that person can serve God with very little self-will. There are different periods in the history of this world. At different times, Jesus sends different graces, always considering the appropriateness of the grace for the time. In other words, Jesus knows what His people require and gives accordingly. At this time, the Lord sees that souls are in distress. The great darkness has obscured the usual process of acceptance for others and many carry heavy burdens that they should have cast off already. There is a preoccupation with self that precludes God's children from considering the struggles of others. This preoccupation has inhibited spiritual healing for many. Jesus wills at this time to send heavenly help that will shake

God's children out of this fog. You have been hurt by others. Heaven knows this. Now it is time to forgive those who have hurt you. Jesus is all mercy, it is true, but God is also all justice. Those who have hurt you will be held accountable. Do you want this? Do you desire it? My friend, nobody escapes divine justice. Where does that fact place you in terms of the sins you have committed? Are you free from sin? Have you hurt anyone in your past? Be honest and I will ask God to illuminate your soul for you because you are in the same boat as those who have hurt you in terms of being held accountable for sins committed. Perhaps you have been injured grievously. Perhaps the evil committed against you far exceeds anything you have ever done wrong. Be at peace. God will make all wrongs right and the ones who hurt you will have to deal with their own process. We are concerned with your growth today and your growth will be stunted if you do not accept forgiveness into your heart. You need bring nothing to this process but willingness. Tell Jesus that you are willing and He will begin His work. If you are not willing, I understand that, also. In that case you must ask Jesus to give you willingness. Jesus loves this prayer. Do not think it makes you unworthy of the process. You say, "Jesus, I am too angry, too hurt. You will have to heal me enough so that I can even allow such a process to begin." The heart of Jesus rejoices in this and He tells the Father that, truly, this is a soul in which He can work. In other words, I am telling you that there is no reason to persist in bitterness. It is time to let it go. We will support you and sustain you.

St. Faustina

My friend, there is great opportunity here. Jesus is promising you that He will assume responsibility for your healing. This is the healing that comes from heaven, the authentic liberation from spiritual and emotional distress. This is not something that is obtainable from a worldly source because only the divine can make these promises and then deliver these graces. I cried many tears on earth. Do not fear tears. Tears provide the soul with moisture which allows for great growth in virtue and holiness. Tears are a sign that healing is taking place. Sometimes tears flow out of the person and with the tears goes the hurt. Good-bye to hurt. Welcome to forgiveness.

What does forgiveness bring? I will tell you. Forgiveness brings peace. Forgiveness brings self-acceptance because you are able to say, "Yes, this bad thing happened to me. Yes, it was hurtful and I suffered pain because of it." Then you stop and say, "No. I will not allow this injury to suffocate the goodness in me. No. I will not allow it to divert me from God's will in my life. I will not behave badly because someone else has behaved badly. If I do so, I am being tricked."

You see, my friend, the path of bitterness leads in the opposite direction of where you must go. Come our way, to heaven, and you will have joy. The enemy seeks to divert you by encouraging you to persist in bitter self-righteousness and indignation. You know that it is not Jesus who advises you to hold on to anger. It is His enemy, who is also your enemy.

St. Faustina

Ask yourself this question. "Am I angry at Jesus?" If you answer, "Yes," you must tell Him and talk about it with Him in the silence of your heart. There is only one combatant here, my friend, because Jesus is most assuredly not angry at you. As such, you are fighting all by yourself. Day after day, you make a case against God, reviewing all of the hurts that God has failed to prevent. You find yourself softening at times, and then you hastily list the wrongs God has committed against you, backing up your case and affirming your decision to ignore God or even work against Him. If you could see me you would see that I am shaking my head sadly. This will never succeed for you. This state of affairs will really have to cease. I would like to say, "Stop this at once," but who am I to give you orders? You would say, "Who is this Faustina who speaks with such authority? Faustina does not understand my pain or she would join me in my anger against God."

You are wrong, of course. I would not join you in your anger against God because I know God. I am united to Jesus in heaven and I am continually suffused with His love for me. At the very same time that I am suffused with His love for me, I am suffused with His love for you because it is all the same love, from the same Source, and it includes us all. Do you understand? Will you try to stay with me while I attempt to explain this to you?

I exist permanently in the heart of God. You exist permanently in the heart of God in that He created you and He cannot fail to love you. He is enamored with every part of you, every characteristic, and every possibility in your future. Your anger, your pain, your sinfulness, in no way diminishes God's love for you. This is not even possible. God will never reject one of His children. It is His children who reject Him. My beloved friend, you are like a small child sitting in a corner at a birthday party with his arms crossed. Will you do this in heaven? Will you come to heaven and refuse to join in our joy? No. You will not. You will have to work through this pain in purgatory. Now, perhaps you are getting angry at me. You say, "More injustice! Faustina is threatening me." I am not threatening you. You are my little brother or sister and God has given me the task of helping you to cast off your bitterness, allowing Him to replace it with His forgiveness. In order to do so I am using the powerful weapon that is the truth. You have a great many friends in heaven and they want you to begin this process now so that you are ready to come straight to heaven when you die in your body. I want this too. Jesus wants this also. We have many people here who are heavily committed to your cause. Won't you come back to completeness now? I love you very much. I know all about heavy burdens that tempt one to bitterness. Sit in silence and we will begin this important work in your soul.

Blessed Mother

I am with you, my child. I am in all of your pain and I understand why you are having difficulty. Heaven sees everything. This fact should only console you because heaven completely accepts humanity. Dear child of my heart, heaven was created for you. Let me repeat that for my little wounded one. God made heaven for you. This is your home. You will come here if you accept Jesus when you die. Accept Him now and you will live out the remainder of your time united to all of us, who seek to save others. I want to explain something to you so that you know that we understand your predicament. Your difficulty in forgiving is understandable. I had to forgive those who crucified my Son. My love for Jesus is combined with my respect for Him and it was this way for me on earth. He always served God's children. He always put the good of humanity first, sacrificing everything for every human being ever created. His love was perfect and perfectly selfless. Yes, I loved Him fully. In His presence I could only melt with the love He exhibited. When He was crucified, and even before that, unjustly castigated and slandered, my heart nearly broke. At His death, My heart stopped as well, in terms of its ability to recover and love. It was only through the grace of the Almighty God, who breathed forgiveness into me, that I was able to continue on in the world without my Son. I am telling you that you should not be ashamed to need God's help in this process. I, also, needed God's help. God placed forgiveness in my heart and He will do the same for you. A final word of love for you is this. Remember that you have hurt our Jesus and Jesus willingly forgives you. Jesus loves you so tenderly. Forgive others as Jesus has forgiven you and you will know heaven's peace. We will help you. I am with you and I will never leave you.

Lay Apostles of Jesus Christ the Returning King

We seek to be united to Jesus in our daily work, and through our vocations, in order to obtain graces for the conversion of sinners. We pledge our allegiance to God the Father. Through our cooperation with the Holy Spirit, we will allow Jesus to flow through us into the world, bringing His light. We do this in union with Mary, our Blessed Mother, with the Communion of Saints, with all of God's holy angels, and with our fellow lay apostles in the world.

As lay apostles of Jesus Christ the Returning King, we agree to adopt the following spiritual practices, as best we can.

1. Allegiance Prayer, along with the Morning Offering and a brief prayer for the Holy Father.

2. One hour of Eucharistic Adoration each week.

3. Participation in a monthly lay apostle prayer group, which includes the Luminous Mysteries of the Holy Rosary, and the reading of the Monthly Message.

4. Monthly Confession.

5. Further, we will follow the example of Jesus Christ as set out in Holy Scripture, treating all others with His patience and kindness.

Promise from Jesus to His Lay Apostles:

May 12, 2005

Your message to souls remains constant. Welcome each soul to the rescue mission. You may assure each lay apostle that just as they concern themselves with My interests, I will concern Myself with theirs. They will be placed in My Sacred Heart and I will defend and protect them. I will also pursue complete conversion of each of their loved ones. So you see, the souls who serve in this rescue mission as My beloved lay apostles will know peace. The world cannot make this promise, as only heaven can bestow peace on a soul. This is truly heaven's mission and I call every one of heaven's children to assist Me. You will be well rewarded, My dear ones.

Allegiance Prayer

Dear God in heaven, I pledge my allegiance to You. I give You my life, my work, and my heart. In turn, give me the grace of obeying Your every direction to the fullest possible extent. Amen.

Morning Offering

O Jesus, through the Immaculate Heart of Mary, I offer You the prayers, works, joys, and sufferings of this day, for all the intentions of Your Sacred Heart, in union with the Holy Sacrifice of the Mass throughout the world, in reparation for my sins, and for the intentions of the Holy Father. Amen.

Five Luminous Mysteries:

1. The Baptism of Jesus
2. The Wedding at Cana
3. The Proclamation of the Kingdom of God
4. The Transfiguration
5. The Institution of the Eucharist

The Volumes

*Direction for Our Times
as given to Anne, a lay apostle*

Volume One:	***Thoughts on Spirituality***
Volume Two:	***Conversations with the Eucharistic Heart of Jesus***
Volume Three:	***God the Father Speaks to His Children*** ***The Blessed Mother Speaks to Her Bishops and Priests***
Volume Four:	***Jesus the King*** ***Heaven Speaks to Priests*** ***Jesus Speaks to Sinners***
Volume Six:	***Heaven Speaks to Families***
Volume Seven:	***Greetings from Heaven***
Volume Nine:	***Angels***
Volume Ten:	***Jesus Speaks to His Apostles***

Volumes Five and Eight will be printed at a later date.

The Volumes are now available in PDF format for free download and printing from our website: www.directionforourtimes.org.
We encourage everyone to print and distribute them.

The Volumes are also available at your local bookstore.

The "Heaven Speaks" Booklets

*Direction for Our Times
as given to Anne, a lay apostle*

The following booklets are available individually from Direction for Our Times:

Heaven Speaks About Abortion
Heaven Speaks About Addictions
Heaven Speaks to Victims of Clerical Abuse
Heaven Speaks to Consecrated Souls
Heaven Speaks About Depression
Heaven Speaks About Divorce
Heaven Speaks to Prisoners
Heaven Speaks to Soldiers
Heaven Speaks About Stress
Heaven Speaks to Young Adults

Heaven Speaks to Those Away from the Church
Heaven Speaks to Those Considering Suicide
Heaven Speaks to Those Who Do Not Know Jesus
Heaven Speaks to Those Who Are Dying
Heaven Speaks to Those Who Experience Tragedy
Heaven Speaks to Those Who Fear Purgatory
Heaven Speaks to Those Who Have Rejected God
Heaven Speaks to Those Who Struggle to Forgive
Heaven Speaks to Those Who Suffer from Financial Need
Heaven Speaks to Parents Who Worry About Their Children's Salvation

All twenty of the "Heaven Speaks" booklets are now available in PDF format for free download and printing from our website www.directionforourtimes.org. We encourage everyone to print and distribute these booklets.

This book is part of a non-profit mission.
Our Lord has requested that we
spread these words internationally.

Please help us.

If you would like to participate,
please contact us at:

Direction for Our Times
9000 West 81st Street
Justice, Illinois 60458

708-496-9300
contactus@directionforourtimes.com
www.directionforourtimes.org

Direction for Our Times Ireland
Drumacarrow
Bailieborough
County Cavan
Republic of Ireland

Phone: 353-(0)42-969-4947 or 353-(0)42-969-4734
Email: contactus@dfot.ie

Jesus gives Anne a message for the
world on the first day of each month.
To receive the monthly messages check
the box on the reply card inside the back
cover or you may access our website at
www.directionforourtimes.org
or call us at 708-496-9300
to be placed on our mailing list.